THE ODYSSEY

by
Homer

Teacher Guide

Written by
Gloria Levine, M. A.

Note

The text used to prepare this guide was the Bantam Classic softcover, translation ©1990 by Allen Mandelbaum. If other editions are used, page references may vary slightly.

Please note: Please assess the appropriateness of this book for the age level and maturity of your students prior to reading and discussing it with your class.

SBN 978-1-56137-760-2

Copyright infringement is a violation of Federal Law.

© 2000, 2004 by Novel Units, Inc., Bulverde, Texas. All rights reserved. No part of this publication may e reproduced, translated, stored in a retrieval system, or transmitted in any way or by any means (electronic, mechanical, photocopying, recording, or otherwise) without prior written permission from ECS Learning ystems, Inc.

hotocopying of student worksheets by a classroom teacher at a non-profit school who has ■urchased this publication for his/her own class is permissible. Reproduction of any part of this ■ublication for an entire school or for a school system, by for-profit institutions and tutoring centers, or for ■ommercial sale is strictly prohibited.

Novel Units is a registered trademark of ECS Learning Systems, Inc.

Printed in the United States of America.

To order, contact your local school supply store, or—

Novel Units, Inc.
P.O. Box 97
Bulverde, TX 78163-0097

Web site: www.novelunits.com

Table of Contents

Overview of the *Odyssey*

The *Odyssey* is considered one of the Western World's fountainheads of literature and culture. The *Odyssey* and its lengthier "prequel," the *Iliad*, are the oldest epic poems in Western literature. Like the Bible, the *Odyssey* is valued for both form and content—for its powerful language and its compelling story. In fact, the *Iliad* and the *Odyssey* were considered sacred by the Greeks—much as the Bible is a piece of literature to which many people today look for information about morality. While the *Iliad* focuses on a few days toward the end of the ten-year Trojan War between the Greeks and the Trojans, the *Odyssey* is about one soldier's homecoming, nineteen years after the end of that war. Whereas the *Iliad* consists of a series of loosely-related incidents based on historical fact, the *Odyssey* pursues a unified plotline with many supernatural elements —and is considered by many to be the first "novel."

It is crucial for readers to remember that the *Odyssey* was originally intended to be heard, not read. Whether or not Homer was a real man is up for debate—although most people believe that he was a real, possibly blind bard who lived around the 8th century B.C. We do know that the *Odyssey* was originally recited orally—by Homer or by a legendary figure or group of people. We aren't sure when it was first written down. Not many people in Homer's time were literate, but it is possible that Homer may have written out the poem himself or had a scribe do it—or it may have been written down only after many years of oral transmission.

We do know that some of what is depicted in the *Iliad* and the *Odyssey* really happened. Archeologists have discovered that ancient Troy did exist (in modern-day Turkey) and that a Trojan War did take place sometime in the early 1100's BC. (The *Odyssey*, like Arthurian legend, tells of a much earlier age—a few hundred years before Homer's lifetime.) Homer took a lot of traditional material—developed by bards over many centuries—and cast it in a unique form. He used a great deal of repetition and formulaic phrasing—largely as a memory aid in the telling of this lengthy poem.

Students today—over 2,000 years after Homer's time—can still find this story an exciting—and sometimes funny—one that is relevant to their lives. This guide is intended to help you to help them find common threads between their world—with its global and ethnic conflicts, gender issues, TV soap operas, and action adventure heroes—and the one that Homer describes.

Plot Summary

Book I: In his invocation, Homer asks the Muse to help him tell the story of Odysseus, who has wandered for many years after the Greeks sacked Troy. The god Poseidon was enraged when Odysseus blinded his son, the Cyclops Polyphémus, and has punished the mortal by preventing him from returning to his beloved home and wife in Ithaca. The goddess Athena has guided Odysseus on his homeward journey and intercedes with Zeus on his behalf at a gathering of the gods held while Poseidon is away.

Odysseus is being kept on an island by Calypso, who promises him immortality if he will be her husband. Zeus agrees to have Hermes (messenger of the gods) go to Calypso and tell her that Odysseus is to be allowed to return home. Athena, meanwhile, goes to Ithaca disguised as Méntës and incites Telémachus to act against his mother's many suitors, who have been brazenly consuming Odysseus' wealth, literally eating and drinking him out of house and home. She advises Telémachus to leave Ithaca in search of his father, beginning with a visit to Nestor, then Menelaús. Telémachus amazes the suitors by showing the spunk to tell them off for being a bunch of freeloaders. At nightfall, Telémachus prepares for sleep and Eurycleia—once Odysseus' faithful nurse, now Telémachus' attendant—folds the young man's tunic.

Book II: Dawn breaks and Telémachus appears and pleads his case before a council of Ithaca's elders. Antínoüs, the most arrogant of the suitors, declares that it is Penelope who is to blame since she has been deceiving the suitors for more than three years. She promised to wed one of them when she had finished weaving a shroud for Odysseus' father, Laértës, but the suitors discovered that she had been unraveling her work each night. Zeus sends an omen—a pair of eagles who glare down at the suitors before clawing each other. An old augur, Halithérses, interprets the sign: Odysseus will return and slaughter the suitors. Athena, disguised as Odysseus' friend, Mentor, chooses a crew and helps Telémachus make secret preparations for his trip. Eurycleia begs Telémachus not to go, lest the suitors plot his murder while he is away, and he makes her promise not to reveal his plan until his mother asks for him. Athena blesses the ship with a brisk wind and Telémachus sails off.

Book III: (In this book, we learn what happened after the end of the *Iliad*—how Troy was won, how various heroes died.) Telémachus arrives in Pylos as the men are sacrificing bulls to Poseidon. Nestor welcomes the guests and Telémachus asks for word of his father. Nestor reveals that after Troy was sacked by the Greeks, Athena stirred up a quarrel between Agamemnon and his brother, Menelaús. Upon returning home, Agamemnon was killed by his wife's lover, Aegísthus, and Agamemnon's son, Oréstes, in turn, killed Aegísthus seven years later. Nestor advises Telémachus to go and see Menelaús, then supervises the sacrifice of a heifer whose horns have been dipped in gold, to please Athena. A chariot is prepared and Nestor's son, Peisístratus takes the reins for the trip to Sparta.

Book IV: The strangers are welcomed by Menelaús, who shares a feast with them and tells of the trials he went through while gathering his treasures. Helen observes that one of the visitors resembles Odysseus and speculates that this may be Odysseus' son. Nestor's son confirms that his traveling companion is, indeed, Telémachus—come to seek advice. Menelaús describes how the Greeks entered the gates of Troy hidden in a huge wooden horse and tells of the fates of several Greek heroes after the Trojan war (confirming what Nestor has said about Agamemnon's death). The gods held Menelaús, later, in Egypt, and he escaped with the help of the daughter of the Old Man of the Sea—but not before the Old Man revealed that Odysseus is being held against his will in the grottoes of Calypso. Menelaús gives Telémachus a mixing bowl as a parting gift. Meanwhile, when the suitors find that Telémachus has gone, they plan to ambush and murder him. After Penelope learns of the suitors' murder plan, she prays to Athena. Eurycleia reveals that she knew about Telémachus's trip and counsels her mistress not to worry Odysseus' father Laértës by telling him. Athena sends a phantom in the form of Penelope's sister to tell her not to worry about Telémachus; her son will return.

Book V: (Odysseus makes his first appearance in this Book.) At Athena's urging, Zeus sends Hermes, messenger of the gods, to notify Calypso that Odysseus is to go home. Calypso isn't happy about losing Odysseus, but she follows orders and sends him off on a makeshift boat toward the island of the good-hearted Phaeácians. On the way, Poseidon—still harboring a grudge about his son's blinding at the hands of Odysseus—stirs up a storm. A nymph, Ino, takes pity on the half-drowned Odysseus and gives him a magic shawl. He makes it to shore and covers himself with leaves.

Book VI: As Odysseus lies sleeping on the riverbank, Athena goes to Nausícaa, the lovely young daughter of the king of the Phaeácians. Athena plants an idea in the sleeping girl's mind: The girl should go to the river and wash her family's fine clothes and the garments she will wear at her as-yet-unplanned wedding. Nausícaa gets her father to prepare a wagon and heads off with her handmaids. The girls wash the clothes, bathe, eat, and begin to play ball. Athena makes the ball fall into the pool. The girls' shouts waken Odysseus, who bursts out of the bushes, frightening the girls off with his filthy appearance. Athena makes sure that Nausícaa stands her ground, though, and Odysseus explains to her that a god has cast him here after nearly drowning him in a stormy sea. Reassured, Nausícaa calls back the other girls who set out fresh clothes and oil for him. He bathes in private and Athena makes him look especially handsome. Nausícaa, of course, starts thinking that someone like Odysseus would make a fine husband. She tells him that she will guide him to town—but she'll drive while he walks with her handmaids so that people don't "talk" about her having found a husband at last. Nausícaa instructs Odysseus to pass by her father's seat and appeal to her mother for help instead, for he's likely to have more luck with her. Nausícaa drives to town and the others follow on foot, stopping at a grove where Odysseus prays to Athena that he might find compassion on this island.

Book VII: Athena wraps Odysseus in a mist so that none of the seafaring Phaeácians will see him and insult him as he goes on his way. She takes on the appearance of a young girl and leads him to the impressive palace, surrounded by fruit trees. He approaches the queen, Arétë, and asks her to give him a crew to take him home. After he drinks and eats, he tells the banquet guests that the gods have put him through many trials. Before leaving, the Phaeácians urge the king to give Odysseus a crew and ship. Odysseus tells Arétë and Alcínoüs how he met their daughter by the river. (He explains that after eight years on the island with Calypso, he was sent on his way home only to undergo a shipwreck engineered by Poseidon; he woke on the shore and met Nausícaa.) The generous royal couple not only promise Odysseus a ship and crew, but Alcínoüs suggests that he would be happy to have Odysseus for a son-in-law, if Odysseus should choose to stay. Odysseus sleeps.

Book VIII: Day breaks and a council is convened; Alcínoüs proposes that Odysseus be given a 52-man crew. While the ship is prepared, a feast is held and the blind bard Demódocus sings about the fate of the Achaeans. Odysseus hides his tears, but Alcínoüs notices. A tournament is held with boxing, jumping, wrestling, racing. Rude Euryalus taunts Odysseus, saying he sure doesn't look like much of an athlete. Odysseus takes up the challenge, amazing everyone with his excellent discus throw (measured by Athena, disguised as a man). Alcínoüs calls for Demódocus to play the harp and the bard sings the story of how Arës cuckolded lame Hepháestus by lying with Hepháestus' wife, Aphrodítë. The enraged husband then went to his forge and made a trap to chain the adulterous pair—finally setting them free at Poseidon's request. The young Phaeácians dance, and gifts are brought to Odysseus: a sword from conciliatory Euryalus, gold, clothing. Everyone feasts and Odysseus asks the bard to sing about the Trojan horse filled with Greeks. Odysseus again weeps as he hears the tale of how the Greeks burst from the horse and sacked Troy. Again the king notices and asks Odysseus who he is, how he strayed off course, where he has been—and why the story of Troy's fall makes him so miserable.

Book IX: (This Book is told by Odysseus.) The stranger reveals that he is Odysseus, son of Laértes, and tells the tale of his trials. From Troy he sailed to Ismarus and sacked the city of the Cíconës (allies of the Trojans, during the war). His men got drunk and didn't get away fast enough; many were killed by the Cíconës. Ten days later the survivors reached the land of the Lotus-Eaters. After they shared their drug-like fruit with Odysseus' men, the forgetful men had to be dragged back to their ships. Next they reached the land of the Cyclops. One of these—Polyphémus—held the men captive in his cave and began to eat them one by one. After plying him with wine, Odysseus blinded the Cyclops with a heated olive-wood stake. Then he and some of his crew escaped by hiding themselves among the Cyclops' rams as they left the cave. As their ship sailed away, Odysseus taunted the Cyclops, who hurled a huge rock at the boat, nearly drowning the men. Foolishly, Odysseus revealed his name to Polyphémus, who prayed to his father Poseidon to make life miserable for Odysseus and his men.

Book X: Next, continues Odysseus, the men landed in Aéolia, where the king of the winds treated them well and gave Odysseus a sack of winds with instructions not to open it, and a free wind, Zephyr, to carry them home. Unfortunately, some of the men got greedy and opened the bag, and a hurricane escaped, sending the ships back to Aéolia. Angered by the crew's disobedience and lack of gratitude, the king wasn't as hospitable this time and drove the men away. Next they reached the city of the Laestrygónians, cannibal giants who destroyed all except Odysseus' ship and ate all of the men except his crew. On he sailed to the island of Aeaéa, where Círcë—goddess proficient in the use of herbs and drugs—turned his men into swine. The god Hermes gave Odysseus a potion to protect him from Círcë's spell and instructed him to share Círcë's bed, which Odysseus did. Círcë changed the swine back into men and they spent a year with her, feasting and enjoying life. When she released them, she told them to visit the house of Hades before returning to Ithaca. At dawn the men set sail—except for young Elpénor who drank too much wine, fell off Círcë's roof, and broke his neck.

Book XI: Odysseus continues his story, telling of how he reached the end of the ocean and sacrificed the ram and ewe Círcë had left them. In Hades, they met the shade of Elpénor who begged for a proper burial. Next came the ghost of Odysseus' mother, Anticleia, and Tirésias, a blind seer who prophesied that Odysseus would make it home—but not before undergoing more hardship—if he and his men left the sacred herds of Hélios the sun-god untouched. Odysseus, he predicted, would lose all of his comrades and return alone to Ithaca, where he would crush his wife's suitors. Then, said the seer, Odysseus should go to a place where people don't know about seafaring and there he should offer Poseidon gifts. Odysseus then questioned the shades of several wives of great lords: Tyro who bore children to Poseidon, Antíopë who bore children to Zeus, Epicástë—mother of Oedipus, who unknowingly married her son. Here Odysseus pauses his tale and Arétë urges all to give Odysseus gifts for his journey. Alcínoüs asks if during his journey to Hades Odysseus encountered any of the men who went with him to Troy. Odysseus replies that after Perséphonë (wife of Hades) scattered the women, Agamemnon came forward and described his murder at the hands of his wife's lover, Aegísthus. Then Achilles approached with Patróclus, Ajax, and Antílochus and asked for news of his son. Odysseus revealed that the son, Neoptólemus, had fought bravely alongside Odysseus after entering Troy in the wooden horse. Ajax, who had committed suicide when Achilles' mother gave Odysseus her dead son's arms, was still angry. Odysseus saw other dead souls, including Minos, Oríon, Títyus, Tántalus, and Sísyphus. The dead let out a terrible cry and Odysseus hurried back to his ship.

Book XII: Odysseus continues with his story. He returned to Círcë's island to give Elpénor a proper burial. Círcë described which paths he should take. She warned Odysseus that he would meet the Sirens, known for their alluring song. Everyone should put wax in his ears. If Odysseus wanted to listen to their singing, he should make sure that his men tied him to the mast first. Next, without arming himself, Odysseus would have to get by vicious Scylla, with her three rows of teeth—and Charybdis, who sucks up sea water three times a day. When they reached the sun-god's island, they should leave his herds untouched. Naturally, Odysseus forgot Círcë's warning and armed himself. Scylla seized and swallowed some of his men. The survivors reached the sun-god's island and of course Odysseus' men eventually went ahead and ate some of the sun-god's finest cattle. When they left, Zeus called up a storm that wrecked the ship and drowned all but Odysseus. On the tenth day, he was cast up on Calypso's isle.

Book XIII: The next morning the Phaeácian chiefs bring their gifts to Odysseus' ship and a bull is sacrificed. The ship sails to Ithaca and the sailors leave a sleeping Odysseus and his gifts on a deserted beach there before heading home. Poseidon, who still has a chip on his shoulder, turns the ship to stone to punish the Phaeácians for helping Odysseus. Observing what has happened to the sailors, the Phaeácians on land offer a sacrifice of twelve bulls and pray to Poseidon to dissuade him from wrapping their city in a mountain mass. Meanwhile Athena wraps Odysseus in mist and appears in the guise of a young man to outline a plan for squashing Penelope's suitors. After hiding his gifts in a cave, she gives him the appearance of an old beggar and sends him off to the swineherd, who has remained faithful all these years, while she goes to Sparta to summon Telémachus, Odysseus' son.

Book XIV: In disguise, Odysseus visits Eumáeus, the loyal swineherd, who welcomes him graciously. Eumáeus tells the stranger how Penelope's arrogant suitors have been consuming his master's goods. Odysseus eats and drinks while planning his revenge. He predicts that Odysseus will return within the year, then spins an elaborate false tale in answer to the swineherd's questions about who he is and where he has been. He claims to have gone from Troy to his home in Crete to Egypt to Phoenicia to Libya to the land of the Thesprotians, where he heard about Odysseus' plan to return to Ithaca. He says he escaped from a crew that clothed him in tatters and tried to enslave him, and ended up on Ithaca's shores—rather than his destination, Dulíchium. After sharing a meal with his host, Odysseus tests the swineherd with a tale to see if the swineherd will get him a cloak—which good Eumáeus does. While the rest sleep near the fire, Eumáeus takes his sword and sits outside to protect his swine.

Book XV: Athena finds Telémachus in Sparta with Nestor's son and suggests that he return home to Ithaca before his mother marries Eurymachus and carries off some of the treasure that is rightfully Telémachus'. Meneláus and Helen give him many beautiful gifts and a sign appears: An eagle flies by with a tame goose in his claws, which Helen interprets to mean that Odysseus will return home and get revenge. Telémachus and Nestor's son head off to Pylos; the two part before reaching the house, because Telémachus doesn't want to be delayed by Nestor's hospitality. Meanwhile, Odysseus tests Eumáeus again to see if he can get an invitation to stay at the farm—which he does. The swineherd then tells the story of his own past: His father ruled two towns in Syria. The Phoenician slave who cared for Eumáeus kidnapped him in exchange for passage back to Phoenicia. Eumáeus was sold to Laértës when the ship stopped in Ithaca. Meanwhile, Telémachus returns and an omen appears: a hawk plucking the feathers from a dove, which a fugitive seer interprets as meaning that Telémachus' rule will be sovereign. Telémachus walks to the farm where good Eumáeus lies sleeping.

Book XVI: Eumáeus welcomes Telémachus joyfully and assures him that Penelope has remained faithful to Odysseus. The swineherd summarizes the story the suppliant (Odysseus) has told and puts him in Telémachus' hands. The latter asks that the swineherd continue to house the stranger, to spare him from insult. Telémachus sends Eumáeus to tell Penelope of his return—and to have her send a secret message to Laértës. Athena tells Odysseus it is time to reveal his identity to his son so they can plan the suitors' downfall together, and restores him to his usual appearance. Telémachus is astonished by the change and after a few moments of disbelief, embraces his father. Odysseus reassures Telémachus that however great the number of suitors is, the two can beat them—with the help of the gods. They decide to test all the men and women to see who remains loyal to Odysseus. The suitors return to Ithaca, foiled in their attempt to ambush Telémachus. Penelope, who has heard of the plan, denounces Antínoüs, the most brazen one in the bunch—reminding him that Odysseus once saved his father's life. Eurymachus speaks out of both sides of his mouth—promising to protect Telémachus out of loyalty to Odysseus, while secretly plotting death for the son of the man who once held him on his knee. Athena turns Odysseus back into an old man and the swineherd returns from his trip to see Penelope.

Book XVII: A new day dawns and Odysseus tells Telémachus he is going to the city to beg. Telémachus returns home to see his mother and tells her about the stranger (the seer, Theoclymenus) whom he has invited into their house. The seer is then fetched and prophesies Odysseus' revenge. Eumáeus and Odysseus run into the nasty goatherd, Melánthius. Odysseus manages to restrain himself as Melánthius insults and kicks him. They reach the house and Odysseus recognizes his old dog, Argos, lying on a dung heap. The dog gives a weak whimper of recognition—drawing a tear from Odysseus—and dies. Odysseus appears in his beggar's guise before the suitors. Some suitors give food to the stranger, but Antínoüs insults him and throws a stool at him. Penelope hopes aloud that those who attack the stranger are themselves killed and asks that the stranger be brought to her so she can ask for news of her husband. Just as she tells the swineherd that Odysseus and his son would get revenge if he were to return home, Telémachus sneezes loudly—which Penelope laughingly takes as a sign that the suitors will all die. Odysseus sends word that he would rather talk to Penelope at nightfall, when he can escape the others' insults. The swineherd returns to his pigs.

Book XVIII: A well-known tramp named Irus challenges Odysseus to a fight. Odysseus delights the suitors by trouncing Irus. He warns Amphínomus, the most righteous of the suitors, to go home before Odysseus returns to Ithaca (but Amphínomus ignores the warning and is later killed by Telémachus). Penelope criticizes her son for allowing the beggar to be mistreated by the suitors. Athena makes Penelope even more beautiful and Penelope demands that the suitors cough up some gifts instead of continuing to take her goods. The gifts start coming in—brooches, robes, earrings, necklaces, and other treasures. Melántho, a shameless handmaid who shared Eurymachus' bed, insults Odysseus and he threatens her in return. Eurymachus taunts Odysseus and throws a footstool at him. Telémachus amazes the suitors by speaking up, suggesting they go home.

Book XIX: Odysseus and Telémachus finalize their plans for revenge. Odysseus tells his son it is time to take all the arms out of the hall and store them inside, telling any curious suitors that the arms will be protected from smoke and drunken revelers. Odysseus ends up sitting by the fire with Penelope. When Melántho abuses him again, he warns her that Odysseus or his son will make wanton maids pay. Penelope, too, rebukes the maid, then questions the stranger about his identity. He turns the conversation around and she ends up telling him how she put off the suitors for over three years by unraveling her weaving—until some of her handmaids revealed the plot. Then Odysseus tells Penelope a false tale of his identity ("Aéthon") and past. Penelope reveals that she plans to test whether he is telling the truth when he says that he welcomed Odysseus to Crete. He passes the test by describing some of his old clothes and predicts that Odysseus will return when the new moon appears. Penelope replies that she doesn't think so—and orders the women to wash the stranger's feet. He requests an old faithful serving woman, knowing that Penelope will send the old nurse who raised him, Eurycleia. He doesn't foresee, however, that she will recognize him when she notices an old scar on his calf—and he threatens to kill her if she reveals his secret. Eurycleia promises to keep silent—and to let Odysseus know which of the women are "true." Penelope tells Odysseus about a dream in which an eagle killed her twenty geese, then told her he represented Odysseus killing the suitors. Penelope explains that dreams passing through the gate of ivory delude us while those coming through horn foretell the truth, and she is not sure if she can trust this dream. She also reveals a plan to test the prowess of the suitors: She will line up Odysseus' twelve axeheads and ask the suitors to try to shoot one shaft through all the hollows with a bow and arrow. Penelope returns to her room and weeps until Athena brings her sleep.

Book XX: The old, devoted housewife Eurynomë brings Odysseus a cloak and he tries to rest, but lies awake thinking about his enemies. He sees the handmaids going on their way to the suitors' beds and considers killing them now, but restrains himself. At dawn, he prays to Zeus for two favorable signs from inside and outside. He is overjoyed to hear thunder on Olympus and an augury from a woman inside (who stops at her mill and says she hopes the thunder is a sign that this will be the final day of the suitors' feasting). Arriving for the feast, Melánthius the goatherd again insults Odysseus. Philótius, the cowherd, arrives and treats the disguised Odysseus respectfully. As the suitors plan to murder Telémachus, an omen appears (an eagle clutching a dove) and Amphinomous suggests they give up their plan. Lawless Ctesíppus hurls an ox hoof at Odysseus, which he dodges. Athena brings a strange fit on the suitors, who laugh, gorge, and cry. The seer Theoclymenus predicts that a fog of evil will soon pass over them, then leaves. The suitors continue trying to provoke Telémachus, but he ignores them, waiting for a sign from his father.

Book XXI: Penelope goes with her women to get the bow and axeheads for the archery test. Telémachus and all of the suitors who try are unable to even string the bow. Meanwhile, Odysseus reveals himself to the swineherd and cowherd and convinces them of his identity by revealing the scar. They embrace him and promise to help him subdue the suitors. Odysseus tells the swineherd to hand him his bow when they return to the hall, and to have the women lock themselves in their chambers and stay there even if they hear men's cries. The cowherd is to bar the gate. Eurymachus fails the test, and Antínoüs suggests that the contest be postponed in honor of Apollo's festival. When Odysseus, still in disguise, asks for a chance, angry Antínoüs says that the stranger must be drunk and tells him to forget it. Penelope intercedes on the stranger's behalf, then goes to her room, at Telémachus' suggestion. Odysseus strings the bow and amazes the suitors by shooting an arrow through all of the twelve holes. He finally gives Telémachus the signal his son has been waiting for.

Book XXII: Throwing off his rags, Odysseus grabs his bow and arrow and begins the slaughter of the suitors. Antínoüs is first to go, then Eurymachus. Telémachus kills Amphínomus. When Melánthius the goatherd fetches Odysseus' hidden arms, the goatherd and swineherd capture him and torture him by hanging him alive from the rafters. Athena appears, disguised as Mentor. Odysseus, Telémachus, the cowherd and the swineherd kill Amphímedon, Polybus and others. Phémius, who had been forced to sing at the suitors' feasts, is spared, as is Medon, who had cared for young Telémachus. The twelve faithless handmaids are hanged by Telémachus, and Melánthius is horribly mutilated by Odysseus' band. The faithful nurse, Eurycleia, fetches sulfur to cleanse the bloodied hall and prepares a fire.

Book XXIII: The old nurse tells Penelope that Odysseus is back, but Penelope is skeptical. They hurry to Telémachus to view the slaughtered and their slaughterers. Odysseus suggests that he and his son plan what to do about the friends and family of the slain who seek revenge. Odysseus proposes that everyone dress up and let the harpist lead them all in a dance so that any passersby will assume that a wedding feast for Penelope is going on. Odysseus is bathed and Athena makes him look especially manly. To test him, Penelope tells the nurse to prepare the bed outside of the bridal room. Odysseus is enraged that someone has apparently torn the bedstead from its base. He made it himself from an olive trunk and built the room around it. The bed would have to have been sawed from the trunk to be moved. Penelope is thrilled that the stranger passed her test and embraces him, for indeed it must be Odysseus, her husband. Odysseus tells Penelope about further trials foreseen by Tirésias when Odysseus went to Hades: He must go with an oar to a land where people know nothing of the sea and offer gifts to Poseidon there. She tells him what a horrible time she has had with the suitors. He tells her the whole story of his travels, from his victory against the Cíconës to the honors he received from the Phaeácians. Both sleep, and Odysseus rises at dawn, instructing Penelope to stay inside with the other women while he goes to see his father.

Book XXIV: Hermes calls the spirits of the dead suitors to follow him to Hades. On the way, Agamemnon talks to Achilles about how the latter died in Troy in battle—a much more noble death than his, at home at the hands of his wife's lover. Achilles received proper funeral rites and his bones now lie with the bones of his friend Patróclus in an urn fashioned by Hepháestus. Amphímedon describes for Agamemnon how he and the other suitors died—and how their bodies now lie unburied. Agamemnon wishes his own wife had been as faithful as Penelope. Meanwhile, Odysseus visits his father, identifying himself as "Epéritus" and spinning a yarn about his past. When he mentions Odysseus in his tale, Laértës sobs, and Odysseus throws down all pretense. They embrace and Odysseus gives these signs: He shows the scar and reminds his father of all that Laértës taught young Odysseus about the family's trees. Laértës rejoices, then starts to worry about the reaction of the suitors' families. Odysseus tells his father to forget his fears. Athena gives the old man new vigor. The faithful old family servant, Dólius, returns from a hard day of farm work and is overjoyed to see Odysseus. Meanwhile, families of the suitors come to claim their dead and swarm around Odysseus' house. Eupeithes, mourning his son, Antínoüs, calls for an attack on Odysseus before he escapes to Pylos. Medon observes that a god guided Odysseus, and Halithérses, the Ithacans' augur, declares that none should now defy Odysseus or grief will come to them. Eupeithes and his supporters ignore the seer and arm themselves. Athena asks Zeus if he plans to reconcile the two sides, and he agrees it would be a good idea. Back at Laértës' house, dinner is over. Odysseus' band arm themselves—including old Laértës and old Dólius. Athena takes on the form of Mentor. Laértës kills Eupeithes before Athena can step in and stop the fight, saying there has been enough killing. Odysseus swoops down, ready for more bloodshed, but he is stopped by Zeus' thunderbolt. A peace pact for all time is sworn among the parties.

Initiating Activities

Choose one or more of the following activities to help "prime" students for the *Odyssey*. Some activities will supply background information that makes the story more comprehensible. Others will help students link the story with background experience and knowledge they already have.

1. **Anticipation Guide:** (*See Novel Units Student Packet, Activity #1*): Students discuss their opinions of statements linked with themes they will meet in the story. For example:
    a) There's no place like home.
    b) Half of the fun of taking a trip is in getting there.
    c) Revenge is sweet.
    d) Hell hath no fury like a woman scorned.
    e) All's fair in love and war.
    f) Good people usually get the reward they deserve.
    g) Real men don't eat quiche.
    h) Absence makes the heart grow fonder.

2. **Video:** To provide background information about the Greeks that will help students understand the *Odyssey*, view
    a) *Homer's Mythology: Tracing a Tradition* (Part 1 looks at Homer's world; Part 2 summarizes and comments on the *Iliad*; Part 3 examines and outlines the *Odyssey*.) Color. 36 minutes. Guidance Associates.
    b) *The Power of Myth* (Joseph Campbell looks at the myths of the past and present.) Color. 6 hours. Mystic Fire/Voyager.
    c) *Light of the Gods* (evolution of Greek art from the late 10th to the early 5th century, BC; filmed on location) Color. 28 minutes. National Gallery of Art.
    d) *Mythology: Gods and Goddesses* (pictorial survey of the Greek and Roman gods and goddesses; retelling of the myths of Zeus, Hera, Poseidon, etc.) Color. 41 minutes. Guidance Associates.

3. **Log:** Have students keep a response log as they read. On one side of the paper, the student summarizes each "Book" of the *Odyssey*. On the other side of the paper, the student reacts to the episode in that Book with comments and questions. ("I don't understand why Odysseus…," "If I were Penelope…," "Telémachus reminds me of…")

4. **Brainstorming:** Tell students that the *Odyssey* is a poem about the long homeward journey of the hero, Odysseus, after the Trojan War. Write the word ODYSSEY on the board and have students brainstorm ideas that come to mind, as you jot these ideas around the central word on the board. (To jog students' thinking you might suggest—synonyms for "odyssey," common reasons for a long journey, famous examples of odysseys, etc.)

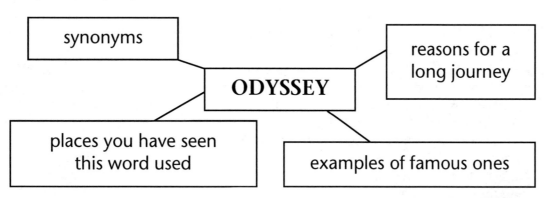

5. **Role-Play:** Have small groups of students improvise skits based on the following situations (analogous to situations in the *Odyssey*). After the parallel situation arises in the poem, have students discuss how their behavior in the role-play situations compares with the characters' behavior:
   - Someone knocks on your door and claims to be a long-lost relative or friend. You haven't seen him/her for 19 years, so how do you "test" whether the person is who he/she claims?
   - You are engaged in some sort of contest (a chess match, a race, etc.). Just when you are about to win, someone tricks you and helps your opponent win.
   - You are being teased by a bully. You know that if you only keep your temper, you'll have your revenge later—and you do…
   - On your way to school, you see something odd. What if this is a sign? You speculate with a friend about what it might mean—and how you'd better act that day.
   - A homeless person sits against a building. Several people pass by; each has a different reaction that says something about what that person is like.

6. **Freewrite:** Write without stopping using the following sentence starters.
   - Freedom…
   - Returning home after being away for a long time…
   - Gods and goddesses are…
   - When you're telling a story out loud…
   - A good leader…
   - Getting back at someone…
   - A hero…
   - Loyalty…

7. **Prereading Discussion Topics**

The Iliad: What happens in the *Iliad*? Who are some of the mortals and gods introduced in the *Iliad*? How does the *Iliad* end? What are some of the themes of the *Iliad*? What would you expect a "sequel" to that story to be like?

The "Hero": What is a hero? What qualities do heroes share? Who are some of your heroes?

Gods and Goddesses: What is a myth? Are myths based on actual happenings? Who are your favorite gods and goddesses? What do you know about Zeus? Poseidon? Hera? Aphrodítë? Athena? Apollo? What is their relation to mortals? Why do they sometimes make life hard for mortals?

The Oral Tradition: What are some examples of stories that were passed down by word of mouth for generation after generation before they were finally written down? Have you ever seen a storyteller in action—or told a story to a group, yourself? What is hard about it? What do you like about it? What are some of the "memory devices" a storyteller might use? How does the storyteller keep the audience's attention?

Loyalty: How much loyalty do you owe your friends? your boss? your nation? What sorts of "debts" do people rack up? Which debts do you think it is important to pay back?

Shame and Guilt: What do these terms mean? How do they differ? Is it bad to feel shame or guilt? What sorts of things make us feel ashamed or guilty? What are some common responses?

8. **Geography:** Have students compare the map that precedes the text of the *Odyssey* with a modern-day map of the Mediterranean region. Have them pinpoint Sparta (where Paris is supposed to have met Helen that fateful day before taking her off to Troy and igniting war). **Ask**—In what country is the site of Troy, today? (Turkey) Remind students that this is the city that was about to fall at the end of the *Iliad*. Have them locate Ithaca, Odysseus' hometown. Tell students that the *Odyssey* is about Odysseus' long journey home after the war. Have them speculate about his route—then trace it as they read the poem.

9. **Related Reading:** Read a few short myths about gods or creatures that appear in the *Odyssey*, such as Zeus, Athena, the Cyclops, and the Sirens.

10. **Preparation for Dramatization:** Tell students that they will be taking turns reading/acting out the story. (Depending on your students' ability levels, you may want to to summarize preselected chapters or parts of chapters, using the plot summary above. Some incidents which work well for dramatizing are:
Book VI—Odysseus awakened by the girls at the riverside; Book VIII—Odysseus provoked by Euryalus at the tournament; Book XI—Odysseus in Hades; Book XII—the Sirens; Calypso; Book XIII—Odysseus appears as a beggar; Book XIV—Odysseus tests Eumáeus; Book XVI—Odysseus reveals himself to Telémachus; Book XVII—Melánthius's taunting, Odysseus' hound Argos, the omen of the sneeze; Book XIX—the nurse washes Odysseus' feet; Book XX—the rudeness of the suitors; Book XXI—the archery test; Book XXIII— reunion of Penelope and Odysseus; Book XXIV—reunion of Laértës and Odysseus; strife and pact between Odysseus and suitors' families

For homework, students should consider what gestures/tones of voice they will use for the scene to be read aloud the next day. (Depending on how much time you have set aside for teaching the *Odyssey*, you might form groups of students and divide the 24 "books"—or a selected sample of these books—among them.)

11. **Listening**: To give the class an overview of the story, listen to an audiotape such as the 24-minute version put out by Spoken Arts ("the saga of the *Odyssey* of Homer told with selections from books 1, 4, 5, 9, 10, 11, 12, 19, 21, 22, 23, and 24"—translated and read by Ennis Rees).

12. **Choral Reading:** Hand out copies of a segment of Odysseus' tale about Scylla and Charybdis as told to the Phaeácians (in Book XII, pages 243–245, "Dear Friends…the saddest sight my eyes have ever seen…"). Have the class stand up and read it aloud together. Discuss what the scene reveals about the story. (What is Odysseus advising his men? How does he feel about them—and they, about him? What seem to be his strengths and weaknesses?) Suggest that students keep their observations in mind as they read the poem.

13. **Overview:** Before your students read the *Odyssey*, consider telling them the basic story (see the summary in this teacher's guide), interspersing key lines from the translation throughout your telling. (Students can be given lines to speak on cue as the story is told.)

14. **Oral Reading:** Choose a pivotal scene from the story (e.g., Book XVI, pp. 317–320 where Telémachus meets "the stranger"—actually his father—in the swineherd's hut).
    a) Photocopy the pages and distribute to small student groups.
    b) Groups should decide which students will play the parts of the characters involved in the scene, and highlight and label with names the lines where the characters speak.
    c) Have students add stage directions to replace sections that would be read by a narrator. (For instance, "Telémachus appears at the door. The swineherd rises to greet him.") Have them block the scene (decide where actors will move, how they will speak their lines).
    d) Have a costume committee (one representative from each group) decide which of several hats best fits each character's personality. (Provide a box of yard sale hats.)
    e) Have each of the groups enact the scene and discuss differences in performance. (How does each performance lend a different interpretation to the meaning/emotions behind the lines?)
    f) Ask students questions of varying difficulty about the scene. (e.g., How does the herdsman seem to feel about his lord? How does the lord treat the stranger? Why does he advise against the stranger's going to town? Why does the stranger say he wishes he were a son of Odysseus?)
    g) Tell students to watch for the scene as they read the poem. (How well does their enactment match the actual situation in the poem?)

Discussion Questions • Vocabulary
Writing Ideas • Activities

Book I, Pages 1–19
Vocabulary

muse	wiles	citadel	transgression
grottoes	versatile	depravity	emissary
malevolent	unstinting	decree	denounce
morose	brouhaha	steward	vexed
recompensed	obstruct	obscurity	gluttony
incensed	marauding	pensive	astute
distaff	clamor	revels	seer

A **recommended strategy** for introducing these and other vocabulary words in the *Odyssey*: Before students have read Book I—

1) List the words and page numbers on the board. (Present the words in isolation.)
2) Have students predict what the words mean.
3) Have student volunteers read aloud the passages in which the words appear. (Present the words in context.)
4) Again have students predict what the words mean—and justify their guesses.
5) Have student volunteers consult a dictionary and read the definitions aloud. (In other words—use a dictionary for verification. Students may need to do additional research to learn the definitions of certain terms.)

Discussion Questions

1. Why wasn't Odysseus able to return home after the end of the Trojan war? (The gods presented him with many trials and made him wander.) Why was Poseidon so angry? (Odysseus had blinded his son.) Who tried to help Odysseus get home? (Athena) What did she do to help? (talked to Zeus about ordering Calypso to free Odysseus)
2. Why did Hermes go to Calypso? (to bear Zeus's message that it was time to let Odysseus go) What was her reaction? (resignation) Would you categorize Calypso as basically a "good" character or an "evil" character?
3. What problem did Telémachus and his mother face in Ithaca? (Suitors were pressuring Penelope to marry them, consuming Odysseus' goods.)
4. Why did Athena—disguised as Méntes—remind Telémachus of "what fame Oréstes gained when he avenged the murder of his father" (page 13)? (Athena was trying to get Telémachus to avenge his father by reminding him of how Oréstes killed his mother's lover, Aegísthus, who had murdered his father, Agamemnon.) Why do you suppose Telémachus hasn't tried to stand up to the suitors so far? (He felt that they would overpower him.) Why did he decide to leave Ithaca? (Athena advised him to search for his father, beginning with a visit to Nestor.)

Research

1. On page 5, Athena mentions that Calypso is Atlas' daughter. What role does Atlas play in myth? (He is the titanic being who was condemned to support the sky forever after the Titans were defeated by the Olympians.)
2. On page 16 Antínoüs snidely hopes aloud that Telémachus never becomes king of Ithaca. What can you learn from this about the political system of Greek city-states at the time of the poem's action? (Rulership was not automatically passed from father to son.)

Literary Analysis: *In Media Res*

Explain that the phrase *in media res* means "in the middle of things" and describes how the *Odyssey*—and most epics—begin. An **epic** is a long narrative poem in elevated style that presents a series of episodes important to the history of a nation or race. The *Iliad* and the *Odyssey* are two of the most important folk epics. Ask students to put the opening lines ("Muse...One man alone was left...") in their own words and to describe the action in the middle of which the poem opens.

Writing Activity

Your job at a city newspaper is to write soap opera summaries for a particular program. Summarize the episode in which Agamemnon is murdered. Write a paragraph of four or five sentences. Don't forget to include the name of the program (one you make up).

Book II, Pages 21–38

Vocabulary

clarion	presage	scepter	pestilence
greaves	guile	hoodwinked	dowry
avengers	requital	raucous	augur
neophyte	beguile	harangues	prudent
tidings	divulges	benign	squalid
marrow	craft	squandered	fleered
plunderers	thongs	keel	libations

Discussion Questions

1. Who was Antínoüs? (the most brazen suitor) How did he blame Penelope? (He said she had led the suitors on, claiming that she would choose one after she finished weaving Laértës shroud—but unraveling it each night.) What would you have done, in her position?
2. What omen did Zeus send? (eagles clawing at each other) How did Halithérses interpret the sign? (Odysseus will return and kill the suitors.) In what other stories have you seen omens like this?
3. What disguise did Athena take on this time? (Odysseus' friend, Mentor) Why, do you suppose? Did Telémachus recognize her? (yes)
4. Why did Telémachus ask Eurycleia not to reveal his plot "till my mother, asking for me, hears that I have gone" (page 36)? (He didn't want her to worry.) How do you think Penelope will react when she finds her son gone?
5. What was the most vivid image, for you, in Book II?

Research
On page 24, why did Peisénor set the scepter in the speaker's hands? (When the herald put this emblem in the speaker's hand, it gave him the right to speak as a public official.)

Writing Activity
Write a résumé for the augur, Halithérses. Include his skills, job experience—and the type of modern job for which he seems most qualified.

Book III, Pages 39–59

Vocabulary

tutelage	aegis	requital	spits
appeased	beseech	discretion	booty
unrelentingly	abyss	clement	sagacity
libeccio	unremitting	pauper	arcade
deity	limpid	unstinting	staves

Discussion Questions

1. What did Nestor tell Telémachus about what happened to Agamemnon and Meneláus? (The brothers had fought; Agamemnon's wife's lover had killed him and been killed in turn by Agamemnon's son.) …about Odysseus' fate? (Nestor said he didn't know.)

2. What was Nestor's advice to Telémachus about whom to visit next? (He advised a trip to Meneláus.) Why did Nestor order the heifer's horns to be dipped in gold before Telémachus left? (as a special gift to please Athena)
3. Who accompanied Telémachus to Sparta? (Nestor's son, Peisístratus) How did they travel? (by chariot)
4. Why did Nestor tell Telémachus, "I do not think that you will prove to be a coward or a clod, if you—so young—can count upon the gods as your companions" (page 54)? (Nestor realized Mentor was really Athena.) Why did he have such faith in Telémachus? (He realized that this goddess was helping Telémachus.)
5. What is one question Book III raises in your mind?

Research
On page 49, Athena points out that "the gods have limits." What was the ancient Greek understanding of the difference between human beings and deities? (The gods belonged to a *different* order of beings from humans—but not necessarily a higher one.)

Writing Activity
You are Telémachus and you keep a dream journal. Describe the dream you have the night after Nestor tells you about the concluding events of the Trojan War.

Book IV, Pages 61–91

Vocabulary

chamberlain	electrum	opulence	tripods
crop	obliterating	stratagem	portico
implore	stalwart	evasive	impedes
snare	brine	flayed	ambrosia
connoisseur	promontory	grottoes	thwarts
galingale	scion	discus	javelin
entreat	stamina	straits	herald
score			

Discussion Questions
1. How did Meneláus treat the two strangers? (graciously) Why do you think Telémachus didn't identify himself in the beginning?
2. What did Meneláus reveal about how the Greeks entered the walls of Troy? (He described how the Greeks had hidden in a huge wooden horse.) Was this described in the *Iliad*? (No, the story ended before this.)

3. Who helped Meneláus escape from Egypt? (the daughter of the Old Man of the Sea) What did the Old Man tell him about Odysseus' whereabouts? (Calypso was holding him against his will on her island.)
4. Back in Ithaca, why did Iphthímë appear to Penelope? (Penelope's sister appeared in spirit to tell Penelope not to worry about her son.) How did Iphthímë try to reassure her? (She said Telémachus would return soon.) Why did she say, "Words empty as the wind are best unsaid" (page 90)? What did Penelope want to hear? (Penelope wanted to hear that Odysseus was safe and would return, but her sister could not say that for sure.)

Research
Nestor's son mentions the cropping of hair in honor of the dead (page 69). What else can you find out about customary funeral rituals at the time?

Writing Activity
Penelope has just learned of the suitors' plans to kill her son. Suppose you are writing a musical adaptation of the *Odyssey*. What song does Penelope sing at this point? (You might take a popular tune and write your own lyrics—or start by writing a poem from her point of view, then set it to music.)

Book V, Pages 93–111

Vocabulary

ambush	decree	makeshift	tern
pernicious	honed	adze	augers
gunwales	withes	halyards	haversack
clement	tutelary	versatile	soliloquy
trident	voracious	breaker	squalid
rapacious	vortex	tenacious	flayed

Discussion Questions
1. What did Zeus mean when he told Athena, "...you can thwart the suitors' plot, so that those baffled men retreat with empty hands" (page 95)? (Athena had it in her power to keep the suitors from ambushing and killing Telémachus.)
2. How did Calypso follow Zeus' orders? (She sent Odysseus on a makeshift boat toward the island of the Phaeácians.) Do you think Odysseus was at all unhappy to say good-bye to Calypso?

3. Why did Poseidon stir up a storm? (He was still angry with Odysseus about Polyphémus.) How did the storm affect Odysseus? (He nearly drowns in the stormy sea.)
4. How did the nymph, Ino, help Odysseus survive? (She gave him a magic shawl which he was to throw aside once he made it to shore.)
5. Does this part of the story remind you of any other stories you know?

Research
Tithónus is mentioned in the Book's opening line, page 95. Find the most famous version of the myth in which the goddess of the dawn wins him the gift of immortality but forgets to ensure that he never grows older. (See Tennyson's poem "Tithónus.")

Literary Analysis: Homeric Epithet
A **Homeric Epithet** is an adjectival phrase so often repeated in connection with a person or thing that it almost becomes a part of the name, like "stout Hermes" (page 99). Have students make a list of other epithets they find in the *Odyssey*.

Writing Activity
Write an alternative ending for this Book. What do you think would have happened if Odysseus hadn't tossed away the shawl the nymph had given him?

Book VI, Pages 113–127

Vocabulary

domineering	indolent	immaculate	cadenced
astute	accord	felicity	base
plenitude	insidiously	insolent	

Discussion Questions
1. Who was Nausícaa? (daughter of Alcínoüs, King of Phaeácia) Why did she decide to go to the riverbank? (Athena planted the idea in her mind that she should wash the family's clothes, especially her own wedding finery.)
2. Who woke up Odysseus? (Nausícaa and the girls playing ball and shouting) Why did they run off when he appeared? (He was naked and covered in brine.) Why did they come back? (Athena gave Nausícaa courage, and she reassured her maids.)
3. Why did Nausícaa trust Odysseus? (He explained that a god had cast him into a stormy sea.) How did his appearance change? (He bathed himself, applied the oil the girls gave him, and was enhanced in appearance by Athena.) What line reveals that Nausícaa wouldn't have minded having Odysseus for a husband? ("Would that my husband were a man like him"—page 124)

4. How did Odysseus find the town? (He followed Nausícaa's wagon on foot.) Why didn't he sit with Nausícaa? (She told him she didn't want the townfolk to talk.) What instructions did she give about how to approach her parents? (She advised Odysseus to go to her mother and ask for help.)
5. Did anything in Book VI make you smile or laugh?

Research
Who are the Graces mentioned on page 115? (goddesses who personify grace and beauty)

Writing Activity
You are Nausícaa. Write a description of Odysseus in your private journal. What does he look like? How do you feel about him? What plans do you have for the next day?

Book VII, Pages 129–142

Vocabulary

prodigious	haughty	revered	frieze
azurite	consummate	edifice	venerable
propitious	tempest		

Discussion Questions
1. Why did Athena wrap Odysseus in a mist? (She didn't want anyone to insult or accost him.)
2. What did Odysseus ask Arété for? (a crew to take him home) Do you think she found him rather bold, for a stranger who had just come to her door? Have she and her husband agreed to give him what he wants? (They agree to give him a crew and ship.)
3. Did Odysseus tell Arété and Alcínoüs the truth about how he met their daughter—and about his past? (Yes—he told them about Calypso, the storm, and meeting Nausícaa on the beach.) Did they trust him? (They seem to.) What about the Phaeácians, in general? (yes)
4. Alcínoüs said, "I would that you, a man so worthy, might agree to be my son-in-law" (page 141). Why do you think this father considered a total stranger good marriage material? (In part due to Athena's influence, Odysseus appeared and sounded worthy.) Do you think Odysseus will be tempted to stay and marry Nausícaa? Do you think Alcínoüs will pressure Odysseus?

5. What do you see in your mind's eye as Odysseus describes for Alcínoüs and Arété how he met their daughter (page 140)? If you were videotaping this section, how would you do it?

Research
Who are the "weavers" mentioned by Alcínoüs (page 137)? (The fates, mythological women who determine the course of one's life by spinning, measuring, cutting thread.)

Writing Activity
Odysseus describes his stay on Calypso's island (page 139). Describe Odysseus—and how he came to the island—from Calypso's point of view.

Book VIII, Pages 143–166

Vocabulary

herald	imposing	rampant	resonating
sinewed	garland	assemblies	deity
inept	prefaced	dalliance	anvil
feigned	ambidextrous	reneges	fervent
vie	scabbard	amity	caldron

Discussion Questions
1. Who was Demódocus? (blind bard) Why did Odysseus weep as he listened to Demódocus at the feast? (He sang about the fate of Odysseus' fellow Greeks.)
2. How did Euryalus provoke Odysseus? (At the tournament, he taunted Odysseus about his seeming lack of prowess.) Why, do you suppose? How did Odysseus respond? (He amazed everyone with his discus throw.)
3. What happened to Arës and Aphrodítë? (They had an affair under the nose of Aphrodítë's husband, the lame smith Hephaestus; the smith then made a device to snare them in the act.) Who told their story? (Demódocus) Do you feel sorry for Hepháestus? Do you find Hermes' comment humorous?
4. Why did Alcínoüs say, "Demódocus must stop at once. His harp is clear and sharp, but what he sings does not please everyone" (page 164)? (He noticed that Odysseus was weeping.) Why did he want to know about Odysseus' people and city? (so he could help him get home) How do Phaeácians serve all men? (by guiding them across the seas) According to Alcínoüs' father, how would this kindness get the Phaeácians in trouble some day? (He predicted that Poseidon would get angry about their practice of lending safe escort to all men, and one day smash their ship and cut them off from the sea.)
5. Are you surprised that Odysseus weeps? Why or why not?

Research
Odysseus mentions the bowman, Philoctétës (page 152). Find out more about how Philoctétës inherited the magical bow. (Sophocles dramatized the story of how he got the bow from Hercules in the play *Philoctétës*.)

Writing Activity
Alcínoüs describes some of the pleasures enjoyed by the Phaeácians (page 153). We also get an idea of what Phaeácian life is like by seeing how Odysseus is treated. Write a letter to Alcínoüs about why you would or would not like to become a citizen of his realm.

Book IX, Pages 167–187

Vocabulary
opulence	skirmish	artisans	hawsers
thwarts	laurels	whey	plaited
plunder	evasiveness	promontory	maw
quiver	pare	withes	shanks

Discussion Questions
1. Who is the narrator for most of Book IX? (Odysseus) What is Odysseus' first stop after Troy? (Ismarus) Why did he go there? (to go on a raid) How did he lose many men? (The Cíconës killed many of Odysseus' drunken men.)
2. How do Odysseus' men become vulnerable in the land of the Lotus Eaters? (After eating the fruit of forgetfulness, they have to be dragged back to their ships.) Does this remind you of any other places you have read about?
3. How did Odysseus lose six men in the land of the Cyclops? (Polyphémus ate them.) How did Odysseus survive? (Odysseus got the Cyclops drunk, blinded him with a sharpened stick, and escaped with several men by holding onto the undersides of the Cyclops' rams.)
4. Who said, "My name is No-one" (page 180)? (Odysseus) How did this prove to be a smart move? (When the Cyclops called for help and said that "no one" was hurting him, the others thought he was acting crazy.) Why did Odysseus later reveal his name? (He got cocky as his ship sailed out of danger.) How did this prove to be a foolish move? (The Cyclops was enraged, and nearly drowned the men by throwing a huge boulder; later, the Cyclops was able to tell his father exactly who had blinded him.)

5. Do you feel at all sorry for Polyphémus? Was Odysseus unfair to him? Does he remind you of any other characters in literature—such as Grendel in *Beowulf*?

Research
Odysseus mentions Cape Maléa (page 171). On a map, find this cape at the southernmost end of Greece.

Writing Activity
Describe what happened in the Cyclops' cave—from Polyphémus' point of view.

Book X, Pages 189–209

Vocabulary

prevailed	staunch	dejected	beguiling
villainy	traverse	flanked	oppressive
casque	malign	sties	wallow
implored	glades	tutelary	impotent
mandrake	ample	insidiously	tempering
lowing	shades	prematurely	cubit
heifer	pyre		

Discussion Questions
1. How did Odysseus and his men end up back in Aéolia soon after leaving it? (The men greedily opened the forbidden bag of winds. A hurricane escaped and blew them back to Aéolia.) Why wasn't the king as hospitable toward them on their return as he had been originally? (The men had disobeyed him.)
2. Who were the Laestrygónians? (cannibal giants) How did Odysseus lose several men in their land? (They destroyed all the ships but one and ate all the men except Odysseus' crew.)
3. How did Círcë treat Odysseus and his men? (She turned the men into swine, then made Odysseus her lover and changed the men back.) How long did they stay with her? (a year) Do you think Odysseus had any affection for her?
4. In what tone do you imagine Círcë telling Odysseus, "Do not spend more time within my house if you will otherwise" (page 206)? (sad, resigned) According to her, where did he need to go next? (Hades) Whom did he need to seek out? (the seer, Tirésias)

5. Why do you think Homer includes Elpénor in the story? Do you feel sorry for him? …find him laughable? How is drinking portrayed in this book? (It gets many into trouble; Elpénor fell off a roof because he was drunk.) What are some reasons for or consequences of drinking in other parts of the poem?

Research
Who is Aeolus (first line of the Book, page 191)—and where does tradition locate his island? (God of the Winds, son of Hippotes; off the north coast of Sicily)

Writing Activity
Compare and contrast Círcë with another enchantress you have met in literature—such as the witch in *Hansel and Gretel*.

Book XI, Pages 211–234

Vocabulary

taut	melancholy	dejected	impudence
winnowing	dejection	illustrious	steadfast
usurped	barren	adept	relented
bartered	astute	ordeals	conniving
distraught	sate	audacious	quest
embellish	ruck	unscathed	bulwark

Discussion Questions
1. Who was the first "shade" Odysseus met in Hades? (Elpénor) What request did he have? (a proper burial) Where else have you seen the dead making this request? (In the *Iliad*, several—such as Patróclus—made this request.)
2. How did Odysseus seem to feel about seeing his mother? (touched, but restrains himself so that he can speak to Tirésias) What had happened to her? (She had died of grief after he left for war and did not return.)
3. What did Tirésias predict? (Odysseus would finally make it home after further hardship.) What advice did he have? (Leave the herds of the sun-god untouched.) Do you think Odysseus and his men will follow the advice?
4. Who are some of the others Odysseus saw in Hades? (the shades of several wives of great lords; some Greeks with whom he'd gone to Troy—Agamemnon, Achilles, Patróclus, Ajax) Which of these have been mentioned earlier in the poem? Which do you know from the *Iliad*?

5. Suppose you were taping a radio play version of this book. What sound effects/music would you use to convey the atmosphere of Hades? How do you feel as you read about Odysseus' journey there? frightened? sad? disgusted?

Research
1. What is a "fan for winnowing" (page 217)? Find a picture. (a tool to separate grain from chaff)
2. Find out what some other storytellers have to say about why Tántalus is being punished, page 232. (See the headnote to Aeschylus' *Oresteia*.)

Writing Activity
Odysseus describes the torment of Tántalus (page 232).
    1. Describe what would be the ultimate torment for you.
    2. Think of a politician you feel has contributed to a problem. Devise a fitting torment for him/her.

Book XII, Pages 235–252

Vocabulary

promontory	putrefying	azure	vortex
burnished	whelp	replete	invincible
dour	beguiling	tribulations	thwarts
pored	holocaust	wanton	pungent
gulled	denounced	portents	amok
vantage			

Discussion Questions
1. Why did Odysseus return to Círcë's island? (to bury Elpénor) What qualities does this show you he has? (loyalty, sense of honor)
2. What warning did Círcë give Odysseus about the Sirens? (not to be lured by their song; stop up the men's ears and if he wanted to listen, instruct them to bind him tightly to the mast) Did he and the men heed her warning? (yes)
3. How did Odysseus lose men to Scylla—despite Círcë's warning? (Odysseus forgot that he wasn't supposed to arm himself, and Scylla swallowed six men.)
4. What did Hélios mean when he cried out, "You, father Zeus…you now must take revenge" (page 249)? (He wanted Zeus to punish Odysseus and his men for eating his cattle.) Why had Odysseus' men ignored Tirésias' warnings? (Their hunger overcame them.) What was the result? (When the men set sail, Zeus called up a storm and all but Odysseus drowned.)

5. Was it Odysseus' fault that all of his men died? Did he feel guilty? Would he have chosen to die with them?

Research

Find out more about the Sirens, page 242. What is shown on the cover? Where would you have to go to find the original artwork in the photograph? (British Museum, London)

Writing Activities

1. Write three newspaper headlines about events in this book.
2. Explain what the expression "Scylla and Charybdis" has come to mean. Describe a situation in your own life that demonstrates this sort of conflict.

Book XIII, Pages 253–270

Vocabulary

keen	fallow	cleaved	amphoras
deride	comply	convoy	oracle
scrupulous	requite	diadem	patrimony
smirched	hind		

Discussion Questions

1. How did Odysseus end up asleep, alone, on Ithaca's shore? (The Phaeácian sailors carried him there because he was asleep, and left for home.)
2. How did Poseidon punish the Phaeácians? (He turned their returning ship to stone.) Why? (Poseidon was angry that they had helped Odysseus.) Do you think they regretted helping Odysseus—or were angry with him?
3. How did Athena disguise herself? (as a young man) Why? (probably to keep the suitors from suspecting the gods' intervention against them) How did she disguise Odysseus? Why? (She made him look like an old beggar so the suitors would be caught unaware.) Where did she send him? (off to the faithful swineherd, Eumáeus)
4. "And I, meanwhile, will go to Sparta, land of lovely women…." (page 269). Why was Athena going there? (to summon Telémachus)
5. If you could ask Odysseus one question about his behavior or thoughts in Book Thirteen, what would it be? Do you think it is a good idea to try to get revenge on the suitors?

Research

Odysseus mentions the Phoenicians (page 264). Find out where Phoenicia was and what it was noted for. (on the Syrian coast; noted for commerce)

Writing Activity

Poseidon causes trouble for the Phaeácians, who were only trying to "do a good deed." Describe a situation—real or imagined—in which a "good Samaritan" ends up with problems of his/her own as a result of trying to help someone else.

Book XIV, pages 271–291

Vocabulary

sows	boars	tirade	seemly
gusto	vagabonds	tidings	concubine
prowess	stint	pretext	stealth
pact	chine	sated	rime

Discussion Questions

1. Who was Eumáeus? (a faithful swineherd serving Odysseus) How did he treat the stranger? (welcomed him warmly, fed him) What does this show you about him? (He is kind, honest.)
2. How can you tell that Odysseus was a convincing storyteller? (He told a long false tale about his past.) Why do you suppose he didn't tell the swineherd the truth about his past? Do you think the swineherd believed him?
3. What sort of "test" did Odysseus make up for the swineherd? (He told a tale about a cloak to see if the swineherd would get him one.) Did Eumáeus "pass"? (yes) Why do you think he didn't just ask for the cloak?
4. "He would not rest far from the boars. He meant to go outdoors" (page 290). Who? (Eumáeus) Why? (He intended to protect them from dogs and men.) What do you think of the rhyme, here? Do you agree with the *New York Times* reviewer who describes the "real poetic power" of this translation and says that the book "is one which no lover of living poetry should miss"? (back cover)
5. Would you rather be Odysseus—or Eumáeus?

Research

Odysseus speaks of Dodóna's oracle (page 284). What was this? (site of the oldest oracle of Zeus; The swishing of oak-leaves was used to interpret the god's utterances.)

Writing Activity
You are Odysseus. Write a note to Eumáeus thanking him for his hospitality.

Book XV, Pages 293–314

Vocabulary

remiss	memento	colonnade	decipher
imperious	cadge	vagrant	solstice
dearth	gewgaws	amber	dispatch
berth	awry	slacked	

Discussion Questions

1. Why did Athena tell Telémachus, "You know what sort of soul a woman's breast may hold: she is so ready to forget a husband who is gone" (page 295)? (She wanted to egg him into returning home.) Was she referring to Penelope in particular? (Penelope had certainly been faithful; perhaps Athena was referring to women in general.) Did her words have the desired effect? (yes)
2. What sign appeared after Meneláus and Helen gave Telémachus the many gifts? (an eagle carrying a goose) How did Helen interpret the sign? (Odysseus would return to Ithaca and take revenge.)
3. According to Eumáeus, how did he end up tending pigs in Ithaca? (The son of a wealthy ruler, he had been kidnapped by the servant who cared for him, who was then killed by Artemis on the way to Phoenicia; he was sold to Laértës when the ship stopped at Ithaca.) Did he seem bitter? (no)
4. How did Telémachus meet Theoclymenus? (The seer claimed that he had killed a kinsman, was running for his life, and needed to board Telémachus's ship.) Are you surprised that Telémachus trusted the stranger? How did the stranger interpret the omen that appeared when Telémachus returned to Ithaca? (He said that the hawk plucking the feathers from the dove meant that Telémachus' rule would soon be sovereign.)
5. If you were illustrating one incident from Book Fifteen, which one would you choose to show? Why?

Research: Where is Hyperesia (page 304)? (town on the Corinthian bay)

Writing Activity: Menaláus tells Telémachus, "All things are best when done without excess" (page 297). Describe what he means in this particular case. Then use two or three examples from your own life to explain why you do or do not agree with him.

Book XVI, Pages 315–333

Vocabulary
stoked	fawned	quandary	dauntless
conspiracy	leagued		

Discussion Questions
1. Under what circumstances did Telémachus first see his father again? (Telémachus went to see the swineherd, who asked him to take the stranger—Odysseus—under his wing.) Was there any flicker of recognition? (no) How did Telémachus treat Odysseus? (He was kind, but admitted he could not protect the stranger properly.)
2. Why did Odysseus reveal himself to his son? (Athena told him it was time, and restored him to his real appearance.) What did they talk about? (They discussed a plan for revenge on the suitors.)
3. Why did Eumáeus go to see Penelope? (Telémachus sent him to tell of her son's return.) Why were the suitors "downcast" after his visit? (They hoped he had already been killed by those who waited to ambush him.)
4. Who was Eurymachus? (a suitor) What was hypocritical about his telling Penelope that "Whoever dares to touch your son will see dark blood—his own" (page 331)? (He promised to defend Telémachus—while planning to kill him.)
5. Is tension high in Book XVI—or would you say there is a "lull" in the action here?

Writing Activity
You are Telémachus. You and your father are making a plan to drive out the suitors. You decide to make a list of the ten key things you need to remember.

Book XVII, Pages 335–358

Vocabulary
grub	overseer	evasive	unerringly
repugnant	fodder	whey	laggard
pelted	bludgeon	staff	prelude
cornices	novice	servitude	planed
wanton	suffice	terse	brusque
misadventures	paltry	paunch	buffeted
revel			

Discussion Questions

1. How did Odysseus (disguised) explain why he was going to the city? (He said he was going to beg.) Who insulted him there? (The goatherd Melánthius kicked him.) How did he react? (restrained himself)
2. Who did Odysseus see lying on a dung heap? (his old dog, Argos) What feelings do you suppose he had? (He wept.)
3. Who was Antínoüs? (the most brash and obnoxious suitor) How did he treat the disguised Odysseus? (He insulted Odysseus, threw a stool at him.)
4. "That is the very sign that death will overtake the suitors one and all," said Penelope (page 356). Why did she interpret the sneeze that way? (She had just told the swineherd that her husband and son would get revenge if Odysseus returned home safely.)
5. Why do you think Homer includes Argos, the dog? Why do you think he has the dog die when he does?

Research

The sneeze (page 356) was considered a sign of good luck. Research the history of other good luck signs.

Writing Activity

You are Odysseus. As you see Argos for the first time in years, many memories pass through your mind. Describe two of these. Then write a poem in memory of your dog.

Book XVIII, Pages 359–376

Vocabulary

insidious	mauled	buffoon	sordid
anoint	judiciously	suasive	torque
braziers	faggots	card	unabashed
scythe	tawny	temples	contentiously

Discussion Questions

1. Who was Irus? (a well-known tramp) Why do you suppose he challenged Odysseus? (Maybe he felt his status threatened by the other "tramp.") What was the outcome? (Odysseus beat him up.)
2. What warning did Odysseus give Amphínomus? (He warned the most righteous of the suitors to go home before Odysseus returned.) What other warnings have gone unheeded in this story?

3. Why do you think Athena chose to enhance Penelope's beauty? What was the result? (The suitors responded eagerly to her demand that they bring her gifts.)
4. How did Melántho and Eurymachus both taunt Odysseus? (The handmaid called him a "scrubby foreigner;" Eurymachus threw a footstool at him.) Why is everyone amazed when Telémachus says, "mistaken men, you're mad; you can't conceal how well you've feasted and how much you've swilled" (page 375)? (They are surprised when he finally stands up for his rights and lets them know they are no longer welcome to sponge off his family.)
5. Why do you think the others taunt Odysseus so much? Is this reaction pretty "typical" even today? How would a fellow student looking as dirty and poorly-dressed as he be treated by your classmates?

Writing Activity
Odysseus restrains himself when the footstool is flung at him. Write a short play about a time—real or imagined—when you were the victim of an unprovoked physical assault (by a sibling, friend, competitor, stranger). Use stage directions and dialogue to show what you did, how you felt, what you said, what you thought, how others reacted.

√ IIII
Book XIX, Pages 377–399

Vocabulary

incites	prodigy	solace	ogle
spurn	hoodwinked	adversity	brooch
malediction	derided	burnished	glen
copse	intoned	besieged	appalled
checked	destiny	ambiguous	disembodied
delude	deft		

Discussion Questions
1. What excuse did Odysseus suggest Telémachus should make if anyone asked why the weapons were being moved? (He should say that the arms needed protection from smoke and that hiding them would prevent drunken mishaps.)
2. What did Penelope tell the disguised Odysseus about her plot to keep the suitors at bay—and how they eventually found out about her deception? (She told him that some of her handmaids revealed her three-year ruse of weaving and unraveling.)
3. How did Odysseus manage to convince Penelope that his false story was true? What true details did he throw in? (He described some clothing she had given him, to convince her that he had really seen Odysseus.)

4. Why didn't Odysseus succeed in fooling the old nurse? (She recognized the scar on his leg.) What does Homer tell us about why Odysseus was given his name, meaning "son of wrath and pain" (page 392)? (His grandfather instructed his mother to name him thus because the grandfather had been enraged by many men and women over the years.)
5. What dream did Penelope reveal to her disguised husband? (She had dreamed that an eagle killed her geese—and then told her he represented Odysseus killing the suitors.) What test did Penelope plan for the suitors? (She planned to have the suitors try to shoot an arrow through twelve axeheads lined up in a row.) Did Odysseus approve of her plan? (yes)
6. What did you like most about Book XIX?

Research
Penelope mentions the daughter of Pandareus (page 386). Find out what the myth says about why Aédon was changed into a nightingale.

Writing Activity
You are the old nurse. Describe your thoughts as you recognize Odysseus—and as he threatens to kill you if you don't keep the secret.

Book XX, Pages 401–434

Vocabulary

untanned	kin	consummate	effaced
millstones	swink	perpetrate	gall
upstarts	fare	oratory	sardonic
flaunt	transgressions	fetid	

Discussion Questions
1. Why did Odysseus, lying awake, grow so angry with the handmaids? (They were engaging in shameless hanky-panky with the suitors.)
2. What two signs did Zeus send Odysseus at dawn? (Outside, there was a thunder clap; inside, a woman commented that she hoped this would be the final day of the suitors' feasting.)
3. How did Melánthius insult Odysseus—again? (called him names, told him to beg elsewhere) How did his behavior contrast with that of Philótius? (The cowherd commented that the stranger had the likeness of a king, made him think of Odysseus' possible misery.)

4. "Athena stirred a fit of unchecked laughter in the suitors...their eyes shed tears" (page 415). How did the seer interpret their strange fit? (He said it meant that a fog of evil would soon pass over them.) Did the suitors heed his warning? (no)
5. Choose one line from Book XX that strikes you somehow—and explain why.

Literary Analysis: Epic

As discussed, an **epic** is an extended narrative poem in elevated or dignified language celebrating the feats of a legendary or traditional hero. Other devices common to many epics include: *the invocation to the muse, epithets, a vast setting, supernatural forces*. Have students locate examples of these devices. Ask students why the *Odyssey* qualifies as an epic poem—and why they think it is considered, even today, to be one of the best examples of the form.

Writing Activity

You are a gossip columnist for the local newspaper, *The Ithaca Tatler*. You waylay Theoclymenus as he's leaving Odysseus' house. Interview him about what's been happening there, and write your column.

Book XXI, Pages 417–434

Vocabulary

trove	pliant	thong	boors
trench	depravity	prate	centaur
chide	pike	papyrus	shaft
socket			

Discussion Questions

1. To whom did Odysseus reveal himself? (to Eumáeus the swineherd and Philóetius the cowherd) Why? (He had seen that he could trust their loyalty.) How did he convince them of who he was? (He revealed his scar.)
2. Who tried to string the bow—and failed? (Telémachus and many of the suitors including Eurymachus and Antínoüs)
3. What instructions were the women given? (Odysseus had the swineherd tell them to stay locked in their chambers and not respond to any cries from without.) Why, do you suppose?
4. Why did Antínoüs say, "It must be wine that wounds your mind" (page 428)? (He couldn't believe that the "beggar" wanted to try the test.) Why didn't he want the stranger to take the archery test? (If the stranger somehow succeeded, the rest would be the laughingstock of all who found out.) How do you suppose the suitors reacted to his attempt? (They were probably astonished.) What do you think happens next?

5. If you were enacting a five-minute dramatization of Book XXI, what would you show—and what would you leave out? Why?

Research
Find out more about Iphitus (page 419), his pursuit of the lost mares—and what finally happened to him, by some accounts.

Writing Activity
Write the inscription for an award to be given to Odysseus after he succeeds at the archery test.

Book XXII, Pages 435–454

Vocabulary
ascribe	compact	recoiled	girt
dexterous	postern	gadfly	bard
tally			

Discussion Questions
1. Which suitor did Odysseus kill first? (Antínoüs) Why, do you suppose? (He was the most arrogant suitor and masterminded the plot to kill Telémachus.)
2. How did the hidden arms end up in the hands of the suitors? (Telémachus accidentally left the door ajar and Melánthius fetched the arms.) Did that worry Odysseus? (Yes, he paled—but didn't panic.)
3. Why did Odysseus give instructions for Melánthius to be tortured and for the handmaids to die a terrible death? Why was he especially angry at these thirteen people? (He was especially enraged by the goatherd and maiden who had insulted him so; he was outraged by the shamelessness of the women who had lain with the suitors.)
4. Telémachus said, "Stop. Do not kill a man who has no guilt. And…that herald always cared for me when I was still a boy" (page 449). On what two men did Telémachus take pity? (the singer, Phémius and the herald, Medon) Did Odysseus show them mercy? (yes) Are you surprised?
5. There are many bloody descriptions of death in this Book. Which one do you find the most gut-wrenching? Why do you suppose Homer goes into such revolting detail?

Writing Activity

There are twelve unfortunate handmaids. Make a list of all the references to "twelve" you can find in the *Odyssey*. Choose one of these references and create a five-frame cartoon that illustrates the scene. Write a caption for each scene and use "bubbles" for dialogue.

Research

Sulfur is used to clean the halls. Find out more about the history of cleansers and disinfectants. Would sulfur have been a good disinfectant?

Book XXIII, Pages 455–469

Vocabulary

reviled   purged   obdurate   begrudged

Discussion Questions

1. After the slaughter, why did Odysseus propose that everyone dance and make merry? (so that outsiders wouldn't suspect the slaughter—but would think that Penelope had chosen a suitor and a wedding feast was underway)
2. How did Penelope test her husband's claim that he was Odysseus? (She implied that her bed could be moved and he knew that this would have required cutting it from the tree which was part of it.) Did it take her long to believe him? (She embraced him quickly after he passed her test.)
3. Why did Odysseus tell Penelope that "there is no delight for you—and none for me—in hearing this just as I heard it from Tirésias" (page 466)? Is the trouble over? (He was about to tell her of the prediction that one further trial awaits him.) Why would Poseidon soften up if Odysseus planted his oar in this place? How would that benefit Poseidon? (When Odysseus finds a place where people don't know about the sea, and plants an oar, he will be expanding Poseidon's territory.)
4. Where does Odysseus head off the next morning? (to the farm to see Laértës) What do you think the reunion with his father will be like?
5. Was Odysseus' reunion with his wife pretty much what you expected—or did it surprise you in any way? Would you have liked to know more about what they said to each other?

Literary Analysis: Homeric Simile

A **simile** is a comparison containing the words "like" or "as." (Example: "My hands are like ice.") A **Homeric simile** is an **epic simile**, an unusually elaborate comparison, that extends through a number of lines.

Sample, page 256: *"Just as, when day is done, a man who longs/for supper after tending two dark oxen/who've drawn his jointed plow through fallow fields/will greet with joy the setting of the sun/and—glad—at last head home/knees weary as he goes: so did Odysseus/welcome the setting of the sun."*

Have students suggest other comparisons Homer might have made, here. Then instruct students to point out other similes in Book XXIII.

Writing Activity

(1) In this book, Odysseus tells Penelope of his many trials. Write down the exact words he may have used to tell Penelope about what happened on Círcë's isle. (Did he tell any outright lies? Did he "sugarcoat" the truth to protect Penelope's feelings?)

(2) Odysseus talks about planting his oar in a place where seafaring is unknown— but this doesn't happen in the poem. Write a stanza about that undertaking.

Book XXIV, Pages 471–491

Vocabulary

bier	unguents	dirge	cairn
skein	scourge	sloth	talents
refute	uncanny	congregated	partisans
reconcile	factions	fray	

Discussion Questions

1. Who did Hermes lead to Hades? (the dead suitors) Why were these spirits uneasy? What remained undone? (Their bodies remained unburied.)

2. Why do you think Odysseus told his father he was "Epéritus" and then told a false tale about his past? What prompted him to reveal himself at last to his father? (He softened when his father wept at the mention of Odysseus' name.)

3. Who was Dólius? (faithful old servant who worked with Laértës on the farm) How did he feel about seeing Odysseus? (overjoyed) Do you think his reaction would be different if he had known that Odysseus and the others had just killed his son and daughter?

4. "But now, do hear my plea: Do not defy him: all you'll reap is grief" (page 488). Who was the augur Halithérses warning? (the suitors' kin and friends) Do you feel any sympathy for them? Did anyone listen? (Some did; others, like Eupeithes—father of Antínoüs—stormed off and were killed.) What finally ended the war? (Odysseus would have continued, but Zeus fired off a thunderbolt.)
5. How do you like the way Homer ends the *Odyssey*? How/where would you have ended it? Some critics have said that the ending seems too "hurried" after the killing of the suitors and the reunion with Penelope. What do you think?

Research
Find out what the term "deus ex machina" means and how the term arose. How does the reconciliation at the end of the poem qualify as "deus ex machina"? (Odysseus is bent on more bloodshed, but Zeus steps in with a thunderbolt and reconciles Odysseus and the suitors' kin.)

Writing Activity
You are designing a video game based on the battle between the suitors' kin and Odysseus' band. Write a brief proposal of what images will be shown on the screen, and what directions will be given to the player(s).

Further Reading:
"*Ithaca*" by Greek-Alexandrine poet Constantine Cavafi
Ulysses by James Joyce
"*Ulysses*" by Tennyson
The Odyssey: A Modern Sequel by Nikos Kazantzakis
The Oxford History of the Classical World, Ed. John Boardman, Jasper Griffin, Oswyn Murray. (good introductory essay on Homer)
The Decipherment of Linear B, John Chadwick. (description of life in pre-Homeric civilization)
Homer's Readers, Howard Clarke. (what is known about the circumstances under which Homer wrote)
An Introduction to Homer, W. A. Camps.
Homer, Jasper Griffin.
Homer and the Oral Tradition, G. S. Kirk.
Homer: A Collection of Critical Essays, Edited by George Steiner and Robert Fagles.
A Companion to Homer, Alan J. B. Wace and Frank H. Stubbings.
Homer on Life and Death, J.Griffin.
In Search of the Trojan War, Michael Wood.
Progress into the Past, W. A. McDonald. (about the unearthing of the Bronze Age city at the site of Troy)

Post-reading Extension and Assessment Activities

Questions for Post-reading Discussion and Writing

1. Which episodes in the *Odyssey* did you find most memorable? most sad? gory? romantic? thought-provoking? exciting? According to a well-known quote, "Even Homer nods." During which Book, if any, did you find yourself "nodding"?

2. What are your impressions of Odysseus? What words would you use to describe him? Does he change over the course of the poem?

3. If you were going to make a half-hour video of the *Odyssey*, which episodes would you include? Why? Who would you cast in the lead roles?

4. With what other classics that you have read would you group the *Odyssey*? Why? If you had to match it up with one other contemporary story (novel, poem, play), which one would you choose? Why?

5. There were many supernatural elements in the story. What were some of these? Of what folktales, fairy tales, and myths did some of these elements remind you?

6. Which character(s) in the story did you want to protect? How did you feel in the final books as Odysseus and Telémachus got their revenge?

7. What questions would you like to ask Odysseus? Penelope? the Cyclops?

8. Which do you think are the most important decisions Odysseus made? Which of these do you think were good ones? Which were not?

9. If you were to give a gift to Odysseus, what would it be? Why?

10. Mark scenes in which Odysseus is displaying admirable traits with a +. Mark scenes in which Odysseus is displaying weakness of some sort with a –. Write an essay on the kind of man Odysseus is and whether or not he would be a friend of yours. Use some of the incidents you marked as supportive evidence.

11. Using a book of quotations, find five quotes that somehow "speak" to the *Odyssey*. (These might be quotes about home, war, marriage, revenge, journeys, etc.) Explain, using examples from the poem why the quotation fits.

12. How are the following themes developed throughout the *Odyssey*: manliness, pride, revenge, sacrifice, compassion, solidarity, war and peace. Provide specific examples and speculate about what Homer is saying about them.

13. Compare and contrast the *Iliad* and the *Odyssey*. Include these points of comparison: setting, plot, main characters, themes, tragedy vs. comedy. Your response might be in (a) chart form, (b) essay form, or (c) humorous form.

14. Write an essay about what an epic is—and why the *Odyssey* is considered one of the finest examples of the form. Start by consulting a reference book such as *A Handbook to Literature*, ed. C. Hugh Holman. Then read some critical commentary, such as *A Companion to Homer* by Alan J. B. Wace and Frank H. Stubbings.
15. Compare and contrast the *Odyssey* and another piece of literature about a hero who takes a long voyage (such as *Sinbad the Sailor* or *Gulliver's Travels*). Are there common themes? similar conflicts? similar characters?
16. Analyze the role of women as portrayed in the *Odyssey*.
17. Write an essay that describes what you learned about the norms governing human relationships in the society described by Homer. For example, what does the *Odyssey* reveal about gift-giving, supplication, privileges, etc.? Provide specific examples.
18. Create a game based on the *Odyssey*. Possibilities: (a) crossword puzzle, (b) word search, (c) "Trivial Pursuit" (e.g., Who was the Cyclops' father? Ans. Poseidon), (d) "Jeopardy" (Categories might include: Gods & Goddesses; Greek Women; Weapons; etc.), (d) "Concentration" game (Put character names on one set of cards, descriptions of the characters on another set of cards. Place all cards face down and then turn over two cards. If they match, keep going; if not, another person gets a turn.)
19. Create a title for each of the Books. The title might summarize the Book, refer to a key incident, or mention the appearance of a new character.
20. Choose one of the statements included in the Anticipation Guide (Prereading Activity #1). Explain how that statement applies to the *Odyssey*.
21. Write an essay in which you defend or refute the following thesis: *The experiences of the voyage itself were more meaningful for Odysseus than his arrival home.*
22. Student essays sometimes contain "bloopers"—erroneous statements that are as funny as they are incorrect. Create a set of "bloopers" that might result from misconceptions about the *Odyssey*. Sample:

    Question: Who was Halithérses?
    Blooper: Halithérses was an old ogre from Ithaca, friend to Odysseus.
    Correct Answer: Halithérses was an old augur, or seer; Book II, p. 28.

    Have a partner correct the "bloopers" by providing the correct paraphrase.
23. Design bumper stickers/slogans for Odysseus, Penelope, Poseidon, Telémachus, Círcë, Polyphémus, Laértës, Eurycleia
24. In recent years, the film industry has been adapting many classics such as Jane Austen's *Sense and Sensibility* and Edith Wharton's *Ethan Frome*. Imagine that the *Odyssey* is to be made into a movie. Complete a news release outlined like the following humorous one imagined by Lewis Beale and Lenore Skenazy (*New York Daily News*, Monday, 11/27/95):

    <u>Why</u> <u>Now?</u> Mediterranean cuisine is in.
    <u>Potential</u> <u>Stars:</u> Schwarzenegger as Odysseus, En Vogue as the Sirens
    <u>High</u> <u>Concept:</u> "Poseidon Adventure" meets "Aliens."
    <u>Boffo</u> <u>Subplot:</u> Penelope (Emma Thompson), Odysseus' wife, with copious spare time, designs world's first pair of Guess jeans.
    <u>Killer</u> <u>Poster</u> <u>Line:</u> Welcome to the cruise from hell!

Language Study
1. Make a list of your favorite "Homeric similes" from the *Odyssey*.
2. Make a list of common words or expressions that have their origins in the names of Greek gods or goddesses or other characters found in the *Odyssey*. (for example hermetically–Hermes; a mentor, teacher–Mentor; tantalize–Tantalus) A helpful resource for this project: *Dictionary of Word Origins* by Joseph T. Shipley.
3. Find another translation such as the one by Richmond Lattimore. Compare a parallel passage in both translations. Which do you prefer—and why?

Drama
Choose your favorite scene from the *Odyssey*, create some simple costumes/props, and stage a "tableau" (with actors frozen in place). Photograph group tableaux and create a bulletin board display. (Some scenes that would work well include: Book VI—Odysseus awakened by the shouts of the girls; Book X—Odysseus meets various characters in Hades; Book XIX—the washing of Odysseus' feet.)

Art
1. Illustrate one of the weapons or other objects described in the poem, such as Odysseus' bow or his and Penelope's olive-tree bed.
2. Create a mobile of items from the *Odyssey* (e.g., Ino's shawl, Laértês' shroud, the stake used to blind the Cyclops, the bag of winds, etc.). Describe the significance of each item. This may done by writing a one-paragraph caption to be posted on the wall near the display, or by labeling each item on the back.
3. Create a symbol for each of the major characters and gods in the *Odyssey*. For example, Zeus' symbol might be a thunderbolt and Penelope's might be her loom.
4. Draw a political cartoon that implies a parallel between a current event and the *Odyssey*. For example, Homer, like modern-day researchers in the field of alcohol abuse, points out the pitfalls of drinking too much.
5. Design a mug for your favorite character (complete with picture and saying).
6. As a group project, create a story map/mural that traces Odysseus' journey. (This could be linear, curving, circular—not necessarily transposed on the geographical route.) Caption and illustrate each key incident as Odysseus makes his way from Troy to Ithaca.
7. Imagine that you are a travel agent. Design a brochure about a trip to the places Odysseus visited. (Do some research to find out about places tourists can actually visit, such as the caves in Ithaca where Odysseus supposedly hid his treasure before returning home.)
8. Show major events in the *Odyssey* on an illustrated time line.

Music
Homer probably told the *Odyssey* to the accompaniment of music. What sorts of music/instruments did a typical Greek bard of his time play? Choose your five favorite scenes and (a) locate recordings of music like that which you think Homer might have used to accompany these scenes and (b) find five pieces of contemporary music which Homer might use today to capture the mood of these scenes.

Research

1. Make a list of Internet sites focusing on the Odyssey. For instance, you can read the entire text—complete with informative hypertext—by looking up this address: **http://www.perseus.tufts,edu/cgi-bin/text?lookup= hom.+od.+1.1** Also, for a searchable archive of 376 classical Greek and Roman texts in English translation complete with user-provided commentary, look up: **http://thetech.mit.edu/Classics/** Please be aware that Web sites change frequently. Use your favorite search engine on the Internet to locate information on these topics.
2. Find photographs of artwork that was created during the Greek Bronze age (the time period Homer's poem describes).You can view vases, urns, jewelry, etc. on the Internet.
3. Research life in Greece during Homer's time. (What was the life of a bard probably like? What was it like to be a woman at that time?)
4. Choose your favorite Homeric god from the *Odyssey*. Examine how that god is portrayed in different myths. For example, you might take a look at the Epic Cycle, a series of shorter epics—which post-dates Homer—designed to fill in the parts of the Trojan saga omitted by Homer. See how Achilles is portrayed there. Find out what scholars have to say about why "Achilles' heel" is not mentioned in the *Iliad* or in the *Odyssey*. (Did Homer choose to ignore the traditional story of how Thetis dipped Achilles in the River Styx? Was Homer ignorant of the story? Was the story simply told after Homer's time?)
5. Choose one of the gods or goddesses in the *Odyssey* and describe him/her. How does he/she display human qualities? How does he/she interfere in the lives of the mortals? Does he/she provide moments of comedy? Is he/she used by Homer to underline the significance of a particular event?
6. Research warfare in ancient Greece. Find out more about pillaging raids (such as those described by Odysseus in Book XXI). What sort of bow did Odysseus bend in his challenge to the suitors? Odysseus' nurse cost twenty oxen. How was the value of captives determined? What do we know about the skirmishing and pillaging mentioned in the *Odyssey*? Nestor asks guests whether they are seafarers or guests. What do we know about piracy and privateering in Homer's time? (*Warfare in Ancient Greece* by Pierre Ducrey; Schocken Books, 1985, is a beautifully-illustrated, informative resource book with which to begin research.)

Current Events

1. Examine how one of the themes or characters in the *Odyssey* appears in popular culture and literature. For example, list recent headlines that refer to incidents or characters in the *Odyssey* (e.g., references to "Scylla and Charybdis" or to various "odysseys"). Which contemporary film/fiction writers have borrowed from the *Odyssey*?
2. Create a bulletin board display of recent news stories that somehow tie in with themes or events in the *Odyssey*—and write a caption that explains the connection in each case.
3. Look through newspapers and news magazines for descriptions of recent warfare. Discuss how the killings are similar to those described in the *Odyssey*. You might also try putting the description into a form like the one Homer might use. For example, discuss how a description of atrocities in Bosnia compares with Homer's description of the slaughter of the suitors and twelve handmaidens.

Notes

© Novel Units, Inc.